Be Alert!

Working while We Wait for Christ's Return

David E. Schroeder

CHRISTIAN PUBLICATIONS, INC.
CAMP HILL, PENNSYLVANIA

Be Alert!

We will turn out the lights on a millennium which began with Anselm trying to reconcile his faith with reason, and will turn on the lights for a millennium trying to find a reason for faith. The second millennium A.D. began with a huge church split, as one side claimed to be Orthodox and the other Catholic. This millennium will end with those groups having splintered into thousands of slivers of Christendom, a Christendom increasingly threatened by the new god called Pluralism.

This millennium will end with those groups having splintered into thousands of slivers of Christendom, a Christendom increasingly threatened by the new god called Pluralism.

During the next two years there will be an enormous fascination with the millennial change. In secular society, there will be a countdown of days and a buildup of apocalyptic fervor. Christians will be churning out eschatological books, articles and messages at an unprecedented rate.

Luke gives us insight into how we as humans often miss "the point." The disciples were with Jesus in the temple in Jerusalem as Jesus was watching the rich people putting their gifts into the temple treasury. Seeing a poor widow put in two pennies, He commented to those around Him, "This poor widow has put in more than all the others. All these people gave their gifts out of their wealth; but she out of her poverty put in all she had to live on" (Luke 21:3-4). No comment from the disciples. Total silence on the topic. Rather, they began to discuss what really turned their heads, "how the temple was adorned with beautiful stones and with gifts dedicated to God" (21:5). Jesus saw the spiritual richness of a widow's poverty; the disciples saw the material wealth of gifts given without sacrifice.

We speculate about the sensational and the dramatic; Jesus wants us to see beneath the superficial to the deeper issues of apocalypse, the revelation of God's purposes.

We have the tendency to see the wrong things as we look toward the future. We speculate about the sensational and the dramatic; Jesus wants us to see beneath the superficial to the deeper issues of apocalypse, the revelation of God's purposes.

The disciples were moved with awe and wonder as they viewed the magnificent architecture and the ornate decoration of the temple. Most of them were country boys, from up north in rural Galilee. They were ooh-ing and ahh-ing at the big building in the city like any group of tourists. And the temple was magnificent!

But now, in a most solemn and emphatic way, while the disciples were admiring it, Jesus predicted the temple's destruction—a total destruction, indicated by Jesus' use of a double negative in Luke 21:6, better translated, "Not one stone will be left upon another which will not be torn down." After they crossed the Kidron Valley and were on the Mount of Olives, the disciples began to ask Him about this.

Notice, from a parallel passage, that they asked two questions: "When will this happen, and what will be the sign of your coming and of the end of the age?" (Matthew 24:3).

The disciples thought they were asking only one question, for surely, they supposed, the destruction of the temple would usher in the Day of the Lord and the return of the Messiah, as foretold by the prophets. Mark's account shows clearly that Jesus distinguished between the two questions, namely: When would the temple be destroyed and when would He return? (See chapter 13.)

The disciples were to receive little comfort as Jesus spoke about the future. To their question about when the temple would be destroyed, Jesus said that it would occur in their generation. He warned them to flee to the mountains when they saw Jerusalem being besieged. It would be a time of punishment, wrath and distress when some people would be slain by the sword and others dispersed as prisoners. The Gentiles would thoroughly trample Jerusalem.

This prophecy of horror came true with a vengeance. The Jewish historian Josephus tells the grisly details which began in A.D. 70 when the armies of Titus, later to become Emperor of Rome, laid siege to Jerusalem. Disease, starvation and slaughter by the sword claimed 1.1 million, while 97,000 were deported as captives. Ghoulish plundering, cannibalism and diets of dung reveal how extreme the situation became. No wonder Jesus spoke with such passion as He urged His followers to flee Jerusalem. Many of the Christians took His advice, fled to the hills and were saved.

In Matthew 24 and in the parallel passage in Mark, Jesus implied that other events would take place in a different era; they are the answer to the question of His return and the end of the age. The Jews would easily identify the words "in those days" with the Old Testament concept of the "Day of the Lord." Three things will occur in those days: 1) Great cosmic upheaval will occur, such as the sun and moon being darkened and stars falling, 2) people will see the Son of Man coming in the clouds and 3) He will send angels to gather His elect.

When will this take place? William Barclay aptly comments:

> Jesus says that He does not know the day or the hour when He will come again. There were things which even He left without questioning in the hand of God. There can be no greater warning and rebuke to those who work out dates and time-tables as to when He will come again. Surely it is nothing less than blasphemy for us to enquire into that of which our Lord consented to be ignorant.

Despite all the information given about the future in the Apocalyptic Discourse (Matthew 24:1-14), the main theme is a warning for Christians to be watchful.

What does it mean for modern disciples to be alert? To watch? To be ready? It certainly does not mean that we should be idle or passive. Paul admonished the Thessalonians about this. Some were convinced that Jesus would return very soon, so they stopped working. Paul warned them that they should keep working and earn their living (2 Thessalonians 3:6-12).

Jesus Himself told us how He expects His people to be watchful:

> Who then is the faithful and wise servant, whom the master has put in charge of the servants in his household to give them their food at the proper time? It will be good for that servant whose master finds him doing so when he returns. (Matthew 24:45-46)

Just what is it, then, that should characterize our alertness?

Be alert to the inscrutability of God.

Among the attributes of God, inscrutability is not one of the more highly celebrated. I can think of no modern praise choruses which croon about God's inscrutability. Nevertheless, He is mysterious, obscure and incomprehensible. Indeed, His ways are past finding out. Just when you think you are beginning to understand God, He shocks you back into humble confusion.

What Jesus told His followers about the temple had them so puzzled, amazed, confused and confounded that they had to wonder whether they knew anything about God at all. Yes, they knew the temple had been destroyed before and that the Jews of the sixth century had been

Just when you think you are beginning to understand God, He shocks you back into humble confusion.

warned not to say, "The temple of the LORD, the temple of the LORD, the temple of the LORD!" (Jeremiah 7:4), depending on it for their security. But this new magnificent structure was not even completed yet, and surely in the midst of a pagan-occupied Promised Land, God Almighty would want to keep His testimony alive by this magnificent monument, the center of His worship.

How often we evangelicals assume we know God's agenda! Surely we know God's mind on all the political, social and moral issues of the day! Surely we understand better than pagan scientists how God has worked in history! Surely we have His heart on how the Church should be run! Surely we know His will about what's best for this nation and this world! Don't we?

Maybe the sin to which we are all most prone is the sin of presumption, the arrogance of claiming far more than God has revealed about Himself and His ways. What is our "temple of the LORD, temple of the LORD, temple of the LORD!" which we hold onto for security, but which God may choose to destroy? An overly rigid theology? Rabid patriotism? The vulnerability of youthfulness? Political "ortho-

Maybe the sin to which we are all most prone is the sin of presumption, the arrogance of claiming far more than God has revealed about Himself and His ways.

doxy"? Sensational reli-gious experiences?

Be careful. Alertness calls us to expect the unexpected from an inscrutable God who will not behave predictably. He will be a stumbling block to belief if your belief has Him penned in your theological cage.

One of the great advantages of gaining a Christian worldview is that it is an open worldview, allowing for ongoing mystery in the universe. Prehistoric life on Mars poses no threat to the Christian, nor do any discoveries of science, nor do any unexplainable phenomena. Our God is an awesome God, and it behooves us to avoid spiritual rigidity.

One of the great advantages of gaining a Christian worldview is that it is an open worldview, allowing for ongoing mystery in the universe.

Be alert to your own skepticism.

Maybe you think Jesus will return at the midnight hour between December 31, 1999 and January 1, 2000—and maybe He will! But more likely, you wonder whether He will ever return. Over 1,900 years have passed since the beginning of the end times, and we do not know how many more years there will be before "those days." Many people scoff at the idea that Jesus will return, or they believe that His promise to return must be understood metaphorically, that perhaps He has already returned in His body the

Church. Peter warned: "In the last days scoffers will come. . . . They will say, 'Where is this "coming" he promised? Ever since our fathers died, everything goes on as it has since the beginning of creation' " (2 Peter 3:3-4).

Scoffers fail to understand that God has a plan, which He has been implementing from the beginning of time, and global evangelization is a big part of it. Scoffers are going to be overtaken by the return of Jesus just like the neighbors of Noah were overtaken by the flood. (See Matthew 24:36-39 and 2 Peter 3:5-6.) We should take no pleasure in that thought. Living as alert disciples means warning the scoffers, convincing them of the reality of God's plan, encouraging them to repent and teaching them to be disciples of Jesus Christ—all the while expecting His return.

As believers we must maintain our spiritual agility, keeping an open mind on inconclusive matters. But regarding biblical truth, God calls us to faith, even in the face of unpopular teachings.

The greatest doctrinal temptation for caring Christians today is to deny the exclusivity of Jesus as God's only way of salvation and to deny that those outside of Jesus will suffer eternal hell.

As believers we must maintain our spiritual agility, keeping an open mind on inconclusive matters.

Disciples of Jesus Christ must be strong in their own knowledge of Him and must be convinced that Jesus is the only Messiah. There is no other way to know God. He could not have made it any clearer: "If you do not believe that I am the one I claim to be, you will indeed die in your sins" (John 8:24).

The smorgasbord approach to religion where you choose what pleases your individual taste will probably continue to grow in our society, but Christianity is not one of the offerings on that menu; Jesus Christ is exclusive, not one of several good alternatives. Modern people do not like such limitations, but people do not set the rules for religion.

As Christ's disciples we must be alert to opportunities to advance His kingdom.

Notice that Jesus did not use the disciples' curiosity to teach them eschatology, but to exhort them about their response to an uncertain future. The disciples were to be preoccupied with alertness and obedience, not future events. After His resurrection and before He ascended, Jesus was asked by His

The greatest doctrinal temptation for caring Christians today is to deny the exclusivity of Jesus as God's only way of salvation and to deny that those outside of Jesus will suffer eternal hell.

disciples, "Lord, are you at this time going to restore the kingdom to Israel?" (Acts 1:6). They were still gripped by eschatology. He replied:

> It is not for you to know the times or dates the Father has set by his own authority. But you will receive power when the Holy Spirit comes on you; and you will be my witnesses in Jerusalem, and in all Judea and Samaria, and to the ends of the earth. (1:7-8)

Jesus wants His people to concentrate on evangelism, not eschatology. He does not require us to figure out the mysteries of the future, but to work to give the future to others.

Jesus wants His people to concentrate on evangelism, not eschatology. He does not require us to figure out the mysteries of the future, but to work to give the future to others.

As disciples of Jesus Christ at the end of the second millennium, we surely must make His last command our first concern because it teaches us to keep an eye on His coming even as we make disciples of the nations. The great missionary movement called The Christian and Missionary Alliance, described by Donald McGavran as "without doubt the leading missionary society of the twentieth century," is fond of the Great Commission, but it was born out of a verse that should be called the Great

Motivation: "And this gospel of the kingdom will be preached in the whole world as a testimony to all nations, and then the end will come" (Matthew 24:14).

It is love for Christ's return which motivates missions. Missions without "Maranatha" is simply religious duty. Those most passionate about missions are those who love His appearing.

It is love for Christ's return which motivates missions. Missions without "Maranatha" is simply religious duty. Those most passionate about missions are those who love His appearing.

We want to see Him vindicated in the sight of all believers and scoffers. We long to see every knee bow before Him and to hear every tongue confess His lordship. But in the meantime, we had better pay heed to the strong words He has given His followers about remaining alert.